BATSFORD'S

Jack the
Ripper's
London

Malcolm Day

BATSFORD

A woman is solicited on a murky night in Victorian London

The poor in Victorian London

In 1888, a series of horrific murders in the East End of London shocked the whole country. They happened at a time when the East End was suffering increasing depredations. Slum clearance in adjacent districts, to make room for new Victorian enterprises such as the great railway stations and imperial docks, meant that the poor had to squeeze into an already crowded East End. Coupled with a sudden influx of Irish immigrants and Jewish refugees from Eastern Europe, this melting pot of the disadvantaged had tipped into a desperate urban squalor.

Pamphlets with titles such as *The Bitter Cry of Outcast London* prompted a rash of parliamentary committees to investigate. In one study, *Life and Labour of the People in London*, the Victorian philanthropist Charles Booth said that the East End had a population of 900,000 at this time and virtually half of them were living in poverty. Many families – whose main breadwinner was lucky if he found occasional work as a labourer – went hungry. They were unable to afford new clothes; children's clothing

Charles Booth

▲ The dwellings of the urban poor in 1875

▼ Back yards and privies in the East End

quickly deteriorated into rags and they usually went about shoeless. An inadequate water supply, pumped directly from the foul River Thames, produced unhygienic conditions and encouraged disease. In a desperate downward spiral, it is not surprising that some men were driven into criminal activity and some women fell into the 'oldest profession': prostitution.

A typical back street of Whitechapel

Whitechapel

At the heart of this East End misery lay the district of Whitechapel, the epitome of all that was filthy about Dickensian London. In *Oliver Twist*, Charles Dickens depicted Whitechapel as a sordid place, where Fagin famously had his lair. His description still held true at the time of the 1888 murders, although it had been written fifty years earlier. The same sinister atmosphere hung heavily over the dark, narrow alleys, which seemed to twist on forever.

The area of the murders

Colloquially, Whitechapel covered a larger area than that set by its parish boundaries, and included Spitalfields and much of Aldgate. Along its southern edge, running east to west, was Commercial Road. In the late 1880s, this was one of the widest roads in London, built with stone tramways on either side to support huge wagons carrying cargo from the docks to the City of London. From this trunk route ran many of the smaller roads that are linked with the Whitechapel murders. Running north to south on the western flank of Whitechapel was Commercial Street, which met Whitechapel High Street at its southern end at Aldgate. Once off these main roads, the pedestrian entered a maze of alleys that stretched beyond the arm of the law.

Whitechapel was the epitome of all that was filthy about Dickensian London

Living conditions

People lived in dank tenement buildings. The homeless and tramps used dosshouses – if they were able to pay for a night's keep. Conditions were cramped and stinking, especially in summer, when a dosshouse dormitory might accommodate 60–80 hot, sweaty bodies. The less fortunate would lay down their head in a doorway or slump against a few stairs, praying that they might pass the night unmolested.

The workhouse was an alternative. Conceived as state-funded shelter for the 'blameless poor', workhouses were usually poorly run and exploitative. In return for working, the destitute received food and a roof over their head. However, a bowl of gruel would be scant reward for a long day's drudgery; conditions were often so harsh and depressing that inmates soon preferred to try their luck back on the streets.

Crime and commerce

Lying outside the jurisdiction of the City of London police, the environs of Whitechapel were perfect for petty criminal activity. Thieves made a living out of training boys as pickpockets, or 'toolers', who would operate by day in wealthier districts where ladies in voluminous crinolines made easy targets. The main business of Whitechapel was the retail of clothing; the rag-and-bone trade was a spin-off from this. The market in Middlesex Street (formerly known as Petticoat Lane) formed the focus for trade. Even today there are dressmakers and haberdashers here selling their wares and skills.

Crime, racism, poverty and depravity were severally blamed for the social unrest that bedevilled the area

In Whitechapel alone, the Metropolitan police estimated there were over 1,200 low-class prostitutes operating and more than 60 brothels. The services of a cheap prostitute in an alley could be bought for 2 or 3 pence, the price of a large glass of gin. Newcomers to the area were quickly sucked into this way of life.

Middlesex Street market

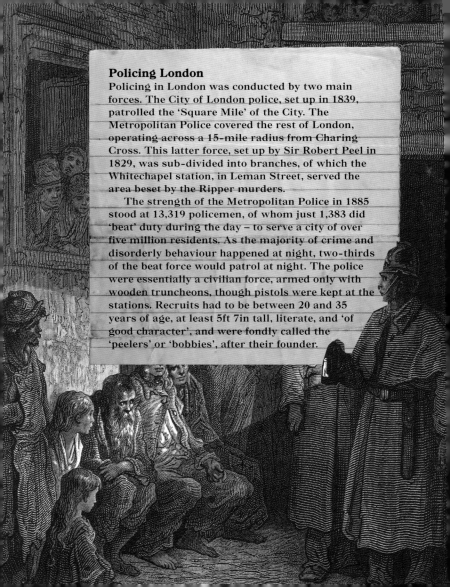

Policing London

Policing in London was conducted by two main forces. The City of London police, set up in 1839, patrolled the 'Square Mile' of the City. The Metropolitan Police covered the rest of London, operating across a 15-mile radius from Charing Cross. This latter force, set up by Sir Robert Peel in 1829, was sub-divided into branches, of which the Whitechapel station, in Leman Street, served the area beset by the Ripper murders.

The strength of the Metropolitan Police in 1885 stood at 13,319 policemen, of whom just 1,383 did 'beat' duty during the day – to serve a city of over five million residents. As the majority of crime and disorderly behaviour happened at night, two-thirds of the beat force would patrol at night. The police were essentially a civilian force, armed only with wooden truncheons, though pistols were kept at the stations. Recruits had to be between 20 and 35 years of age, at least 5ft 7in tall, literate, and 'of good character', and were fondly called the 'peelers' or 'bobbies', after their founder.

This melting pot of the disadvantaged had tipped into a desperate urban squalor

Social unrest

The economic hardship made worse by immigration to the area increased social tensions. In the two years prior to the murders there were several demonstrations and riots, which culminated on 13 November 1887 in what came to be known as Bloody Sunday. Demonstrations by unemployed workers had been increasing; they were focused on the East End, where there was a large working-class community. Irish labourers in Whitechapel stoked the flames of discontent with their own grievances about Home Rule for their country. Fabian socialists – led by George Bernard Shaw among others – and proponents of Home Rule joined forces in a march from the East End to Trafalgar Square. Violent clashes with the police resulted in many injuries, even deaths.

Whitechapel in the headlines

Although this protest had no direct link with the Whitechapel murders of the following year, the event attracted media attention to the East End, with all its social problems. Crime, racism, poverty and depravity were severally blamed for the social unrest that bedevilled the area. By the summer of 1888, the place was already a den of iniquity in the eyes of the reading public. It also meant that Whitechapel was ripe for some pretty lurid speculation by the Victorian press when a series of grotesque murders all happened within an area of one mile and were attributed to one 'Jack the Ripper'.

Emma Smith

Brick Lane was a quiet, though not entirely cheerless, road running north to south through Whitechapel. Emma Smith was a 45-year-old prostitute who claimed to have fallen on hard times, a habitual drunk since her husband 'left' her – whether he left for other pastures or whether he left this world, we are unsure. Despite unruly behaviour, she followed an unwavering daily routine. Every evening, between 6 pm and 7 pm, Emma would leave her lodgings at 18 George Street and ply her trade through the night until the small hours of the following morning, when she would return home. So it was on the night of Easter Monday, 3 April 1888. Having left home at around 6 pm, she was seen much later, at 12.15 am, in Farrance Street, Limehouse, with a man dressed in dark clothes and a white scarf.

The attack

The next time she was seen was four hours later, staggering home in a distraught state, bleeding heavily from between her legs. The lodging house deputy, Mary Russell, and lodger Annie Lee rushed her to the London

Hospital on Whitechapel Road, where a surgeon endeavoured to save her. While still conscious, Emma told the story of her assault. A gang of three or four youths had followed her from Whitechapel Church before setting upon her, beating and raping her, and finally rupturing her perineum with a blunt instrument. On finishing her description, she fell into a coma and died four days later.

Roving gangs were a known menace in the area. They preyed on defenceless prostitutes, extorting their night's earnings in return for protection. Emma was probably unwilling to part with her cash and paid the price. However, this murder is not thought to be the work of Jack the Ripper, who operated alone. Rape was also not his style. The murder received scant attention in the press until September, when the case was wrongly attributed to the Ripper.

Martha Tabram

A few months later, another incident happened in Whitechapel. Again it involved a woman who liked her drink and funded the habit through prostitution. Martha Tabram (née White) was married to Henry Tabram for six years. Since the marriage ended she had sustained a rocky relationship with a carpenter, Henry Turner, while also trying to bring up two sons. Martha tended to stay out late at night, sometimes not returning until early in the morning. The couple lodged at 4 Star Place, on Commercial Road, with a Mrs Mary Bousfield; she described Martha as a woman who 'preferred a glass of ale to a cup of tea'. Forced by rent arrears to quit the premises, the couple went their separate ways in July 1888.

The Ten Bells was frequented by the Ripper's victims

Prostitution

The middle-aged Martha eked out a living as best she could, selling trinkets and working as a prostitute. Her last known address was 19 George Street, Spitalfields. The last time Turner saw her, on 4 August, she was destitute in Leadenhall Street, near Aldgate pump. He gave her 1 shilling and sixpence so she could try to do some business buying and selling trinkets.

On Bank Holiday Monday, 6 August, she and a friend, Mary Ann Connelly, known as Pearly Poll, spent the evening together in a number of pubs.

Pubs in Whitechapel

One of the few outlets for a spot of relaxation and pleasure in the Victorian East End was the public house, or pub. They provided warmth, a sociable atmosphere, and, in a time when water was unsafe, ale to quench thirst. There were half a dozen drinking holes in Whitechapel and men and women of all ages, even children, would go there. Ale, porter, wine and gin for the middle-aged 'soakers' were sold. Two or three pennies would buy a large glass of gin. Some customers might stay all day and night, for licences within the Metropolitan area allowed 20 and a half hours opening per day. Not surprisingly, pubs frequently became rowdy, even riotous. Brawls were not uncommon.

Intoxicated men were also fair game for business from the one class of women who most frequented pubs: prostitutes. They would walk from one tavern to another looking out for likely clients. We know, for instance, that the Ripper victim Mary Kelly visited at least three pubs on her last night: The Ten Bells, probably the most popular in Whitechapel, The Horn of Plenty and The Britannia. Others in the district included The Alma, The King's Stores and The City Darts (formerly The Princess Alice).

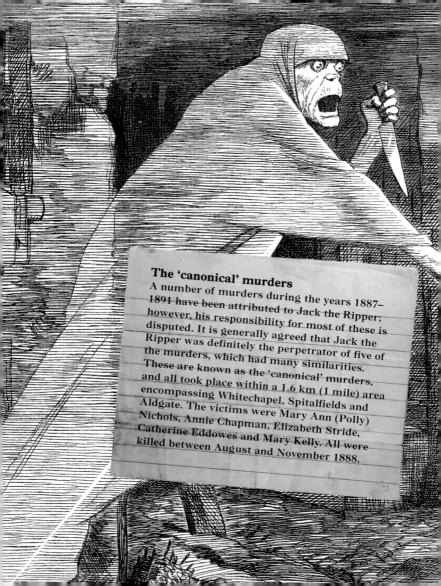

The 'canonical' murders

A number of murders during the years 1887–1891 have been attributed to Jack the Ripper; however, his responsibility for most of these is disputed. It is generally agreed that Jack the Ripper was definitely the perpetrator of five of the murders, which had many similarities. These are known as the 'canonical' murders, and all took place within a 1.6 km (1 mile) area encompassing Whitechapel, Spitalfields and Aldgate. The victims were Mary Ann (Polly) Nichols, Annie Chapman, Elizabeth Stride, Catherine Eddowes and Mary Kelly. All were killed between August and November 1888.

They usually found themselves in the company of soldiers. Mary Ann later said that they picked up two guardsmen and went on a pub crawl that included the White Swan on Whitechapel High Street. Close to midnight, the two women went their separate ways to be alone with their partners. Mary Ann went into Angel Alley, while Martha walked into George Yard (now Gunthorpe Street).

The murderer strikes

At about 2 am, a policeman on the beat saw a Grenadier Guardsman loitering in George Yard, who said he was 'waiting for a chum who had gone off with a girl'. An hour and a half later a resident at George Yard Buildings, Albert Crow, returned home from his work as a carman (driver of a cab or cart) and noticed a tramp 'asleep' on the first floor landing. He didn't think anything of it, as such a sight was quite common. But an hour later, in better light, another resident, John Reeves, noticed the body of Martha amid a pool of blood, whereupon he fetched the police. She lay on her back, arms at her sides, with fists clenched, and legs spread out.

The post-mortem examination revealed multiple stab wounds, including some caused by a dagger or bayonet. Identity parades failed to nail the killer. The only man thought by Pearly Poll to resemble her dead friend's companion had an alibi. So the murder remains a mystery. Some students of Ripper cases ('Ripperologists') reckon this to be the first of his murders. But the use of a bayonet is inconsistent with the style of the five later murders that are attributed to Jack the Ripper and which came to be known as the 'canonical' murders.

> **She lay on her back, arms at her sides, with fists clenched, and legs spread out**

Mary Ann (Polly) Nichols

The first accepted victim of Jack the Ripper was a small, brown-eyed woman in her mid-forties, though generally thought to look young for her age. A friend described her as 'a very clean woman who always seemed to keep to herself'. She was also an alcoholic.

Mary Ann (also known as Polly) Walker married William Nichols in 1864 and had five children by him. The relationship had its ups and downs, and in 1881 they separated for the last time. About a year later, William discovered that Polly was living as a prostitute and he cut off support payments to her. Polly was forced to live in workhouses through most of the 1880s.

A job in service

On 12 May 1888, Polly left Lambeth workhouse to become a domestic servant for Samuel and Sarah Cowdry, who had applied to the workhouse with the vacancy. The Cowdrys lived in the upmarket suburb of Wandsworth, and for the brief time Polly was there she seemed to be proud of herself, writing to her father:

'I just right [sic] to say you will be glad to know that I am settled in my new place, and going all right up to now. My people went out yesterday and have not returned, so I am left in charge. It is a grand place inside, with trees and gardens back and front. All has been newly done up. They are teetotallers and religious so I ought to get on. They are very nice people and I have not too much to do. I hope you are all right and the boy [her eldest son] has work. So good bye for the present.

From yours truly,
Polly.'

This was the last letter Polly sent her father. She worked there for two more months before leaving, making off with cloth worth £3 10s.

A policeman investigates the body of Polly Nichols

Back on the streets

Polly went back to the East End, finding lodgings at 18 Thrawl Street, Spitalfields, where she shared a room with four women. Then, on 24 August, she moved to her final lodgings at the White House at 56 Flower and Dean Street, a much seedier place where men and women were allowed to sleep together.

On the night of Thursday 30 August, Polly spent the evening at the Frying Pan pub on the corner of Thrawl Street and Brick Lane, returning to her lodgings early on the morning of Friday 31 August at about 12.30 am. But an hour later, the deputy of the lodgings told her to leave because she couldn't pay her doss money. Polly left the premises in a defiant mood, claiming that she would soon be back with the money because she was donning a fine black velvet bonnet. While out, Polly met her friend Emily Holland outside a grocer's shop on the corner of Osborn Street and Whitechapel Road. There they chatted for a while, Emily noting that Polly 'was very drunk and staggered against the wall'. Polly said she had made and spent her doss money three times that day and would get some more. And with that, she went off eastwards down Whitechapel Road. That was the last time anyone saw Polly alive.

Site of the Ripper's murder of Polly Nichols

The only illumination was from a single gas lamp at the far end of the street

HE SAW A BODY ON THE PAVEMENT.

Slashed open

Polly's body was found at about 3.45 am in Buck's Row, some ten minutes from Osborn Street, by a carman on his way to work in the City Road. The police were alerted and a doctor living nearby ministered to the body but pronounced her dead by only a few minutes. Polly had had her throat cut and her lower abdomen viciously ripped open with a long blade. Although people lived close by and the road was on a policeman's beat, no one had heard a sound. The subtle mystery of the Ripper murders had begun.

Depiction of the body's discovery in a popular magazine

Annie Chapman

Jack the Ripper's second victim fell a little over a week later, only 0.8 km (½ mile) away from where Polly Nichols was found. This woman, Annie Chapman, spent the early part of her marriage living in well-to-do places in west London and in Windsor where her husband, John Chapman, was employed as a coachman. They had three children; the youngest was disabled and, following the usual custom, was sent away to a home. The eldest, Emily, died of meningitis aged 12.

Annie was short and stout, with blue eyes and dark, wavy hair. Her friend Amelia, a packing-case maker, described her as a 'sober, steady-going woman who seldom took any drink'. However, she did drink, and easily lost control – in Windsor she was arrested for drunkenness several times. Her life declined considerably after her husband died in 1886. They had separated a year or two before that, but now she would no longer receive his support payment of 10 shillings a week, which she had supplemented by doing crochet-work and selling flowers.

Annie Chapman

The fateful encounter

Her husband's death forced Annie into the precarious
life of a prostitute. In the summer of 1888 she lived at
Crossingham's Lodging House at 35 Dorset Street,
Spitalfields, which accommodated about 300 people.
'I haven't sufficient money for my bed,' she told the
house deputy on the night of Friday 7 September, 'but
don't let it. I shall not be long before I'm in.' With
that, she left the building at 1.30 am dressed in a long,
shaped black coat, red and white stockings, laced boots
and a white neckerchief. She walked into Little
Paternoster Row, heading towards Brushfield Street
and on to Spitalfields market.

Some hours later, at 5.30 am, a witness named
Elizabeth Long said she saw Annie Chapman talking
with a man of 'shabby-genteel' appearance, standing
against the shutters outside 29 Hanbury Street. A few
minutes later, a young carpenter living next door, at
number 27, walked into his backyard, possibly to use
the outdoor privy, and heard voices from the other side
of the boundary fence. All he could make out was a
woman saying 'No!', followed by the sound of
something falling against the fence. Annie's body was
discovered about 6 am by a carman who lived with his
family on the third floor of number 29. He went to
alert the police at Commercial Street police station.

Present location of
Chapman's murder

The body of Annie
Chapman

A monstrous murder

Annie's throat had been cut deeply, her neckerchief partly obscuring it. Dr George Phillips described the body as he found it: 'The left arm was placed across the left breast. The legs were drawn up, the feet resting on the ground, and the knees turned outwards … The body was terribly mutilated …' Her abdomen had been ripped open with a very sharp knife, and the intestines lifted out and dumped on the right shoulder of the victim, as though to put them out of the way of the pelvic organs, which had been removed and were nowhere to be seen. In the opinion of the post-mortem examiners, the murderer used the sort of knife that a surgeon might possess, and certainly the incisions indicated anatomical knowledge.

The sheer horror of this murder sent the local community reeling in a frenzy of fear. This killing was neither a *crime passionnel*, nor the result of a jealous rage, nor even a murder for money, which would have been bad enough. This was something unknown – a cold-blooded, gratuitous act of brutality that smacked of a madman who was stalking the streets of Whitechapel after dark. By day, the locals met and speculated about who could be the monster in their midst.

First suspect: 'Leather Apron'

The press, of course, were not slow to carry out their own investigations. Reporters of the *Star* newspaper revealed a commonly held fear of a certain slipper-maker in the Whitechapel area, who was known as 'Leather Apron'. He was about 1.6 m (5 ft 4 in) tall, with black, close-cropped hair, a neat moustache, and aged between 38 and 40. Women who encountered him described an evil expression with small, glittering eyes and lips slightly parted in a menacing grin.

A Polish-Jewish bootmaker named John Pizer fitted some elements of the description and sometimes went home wearing the leather apron he used at work. After the murder of Annie Chapman, the police went to his home at 22 Mulberry Street and arrested him. However, upon interrogation Pizer maintained that he had not worn the apron for some time, as he had been out of work. His alibis could not be faulted and he was soon released, though fear of mob retribution made him stay behind locked doors.

The press make a special announcement

The police are stumped

Some two weeks of investigations by the Whitechapel branch of the Metropolitan police made little progress in catching the murderer. Claims and counter-claims from the public sent the police scurrying this way and that in a whirl of exasperation. Meanwhile fear settled on the community: people held their breath, anticipating more dreadful news at any moment. By nightfall, the streets had emptied except for constables on the beat and those prostitutes with no doss money forced to ply their trade even in these dangerous circumstances. Most tried to keep to the well-lit streets. Some pranksters pretended to be Jack the Ripper and crept up on these vulnerable women, waving long knives under their noses and making the poor creatures jump out of their skins with fright.

Sketches of police arrests and identity parades

The 'Dear Boss' letter

On 27 September 1888, the following letter dropped on to the editor's desk at the Central News Agency. It was the first of its kind to be signed by Jack the Ripper, and was addressed sarcastically to 'Dear Boss'.

'Dear Boss,

I keep on hearing the police have caught me but they wont fix me just yet. I have laughed when they look so clever and talk about being on the right track. That joke about Leather Apron gave me real fits. I am down on whores and I shant quit ripping them till I do get buckled. Grand work the last job was. I gave the lady no time to squeal. How can they catch me now. I love my work and want to start again. You will soon hear of me with my funny little games. I saved some of the proper red stuff in a ginger beer bottle over the last job to write with but it went thick like glue and I cant use it. Red ink is fit enough I hope ha. ha. The next job I do I shall clip the ladys ears off and send to the police officers just for jolly wouldn't you. Keep this letter back till I do a bit more work, then give it out straight. My knife's so nice and sharp I want to get to work right away if I get a chance. Good luck.

Yours truly
Jack the Ripper
Dont mind me giving the trade name
PS Wasnt good enough to post this before I got all the red ink off my hands curse it
No luck yet. They say I'm a doctor now ha ha.'

The letter was at first thought to be a hoax. The police had received all manner of correspondence – rough notes, postcards, proper letters – from individuals purporting to be the murderer. However, the double murder, a few days later, of Elizabeth Stride and Catherine Eddowes made them think again, especially as a severed portion of the latter's earlobe seemed to fulfil the letter's ghastly prediction.

25

Elizabeth Stride,
second victim

Elizabeth Stride

Elizabeth Stride, known as 'Long Liz' on account of her height, was Swedish. She arrived in London in 1866 'in the service of a foreign gentleman', and lived in Hyde Park. In 1869 she married John Stride and moved to Poplar. Her husband died in 1884 of heart disease (not – as she claimed – in a steamer accident on the River Thames which killed 600–700 passengers). From 1885 she lived with a man named Michael Kidney, a waterside labourer, though it was a rocky relationship. She would sometimes leave and be found wandering the streets. The Swedish church gave her alms and she was admitted into Poplar workhouse on occasions. Eight times she was convicted of being drunk and disorderly; the Queen's Head pub on Commercial Street was one of her haunts.

Meeting Dr Barnardo

In the days leading up to her death, Liz stayed at a lodging house at 32 Flower and Dean Street (curiously, the same street where the first Ripper victim, Polly Nichols, lived). Shortly before her murder, Liz was interviewed by the famous philanthropist Dr Thomas Barnardo, who had come into the lodging house to research his scheme of building a home for orphaned children. The women there, he later said, were all terrified of the Ripper.

Dr Thomas
Barnardo

The courtyard where the body of 'Long Liz' was found

The murder site of Liz Stride today

Client or suspect?

At 11 pm on Sunday 30 September, two labourers entered the Bricklayer's Arms on Settles Street (running north off Commercial Road) and saw Liz about to leave with a man on her arm. It was raining heavily and the couple dallied in the doorway for a while, kissing. Her man was short with a moustache, and respectably dressed in a morning suit and billycock hat. The two labourers knew Liz and joked with her, saying: 'That's Leather Apron getting round you!', at which point the couple moved off into the night.

Two other independent witnesses saw Liz later that night in Berner Street, where she was to die. Each described her talking to a man, though the descriptions did not match.

The body in the yard

At 1 am a jewellery salesman, Louis Diemschutz, drove his pony and cart into Dutfield's Yard (named after Arthur Dutfield, a cart manufacturer, who owned these premises, which were located at 40 Berner Street, now

> **'He was hugging and kissing her, and he seemed a respectably dressed man; we were rather astonished at the way he was going on at the woman'**
>
> J. Best, labourer in the Bricklayer's Arms

renamed Henriques Street). Immediately on entering the gateway, his pony shied as though an obstacle blocked its way. Inching forward, Diemschutz discovered that the obstacle was a human body. He rushed to get help from an entertainment club over the road, the International Working Men's Educational Club, a radical organization much disliked by locals for its revolutionary ideas. On returning, the jeweller and assistants discovered that the woman had had her throat slit. It was Liz Stride. Later, Dr Barnardo recognized the face as belonging to one of the women he had talked to in the kitchen at 32 Flower and Dean Street.

Trigger for a second murder
The body had not suffered mutilations, as previous victims had done. It is thought that Diemschutz's arrival had probably disturbed the Ripper and he slipped away before finishing the job. The possible frustration of this interruption may well account for the fact that it was very soon afterwards that the Ripper dispatched his fourth victim, Catherine Eddowes.

Catherine Eddowes

Catherine Eddowes

The pattern of behaviour of the fourth victim of Jack the Ripper was somewhat similar to that of earlier victims, though Catherine Eddowes was much less of a drinker. Indeed, up to the last night of her life, she had maintained a good reputation as an upright woman who rarely got drunk. Just two days before her miserable end, Catherine returned from hop-picking in Kent with her partner John Kelly. They were not able to find sleeping quarters together.

Chatting to a killer

By some misfortune, Catherine became embroiled in a quarrel outside 29 Aldgate High Street on Sunday evening, 30 September. As this address fell within the boundary of the City, it was a City police constable who apprehended her, and seeing that she was drunk and insensible, took her off to Bishopsgate police station to sober up. She was then allowed to leave just before 1 am. She headed back towards Aldgate High Street, turned down Houndsditch, and went along Duke Street and Church Passage and into Mitre Square. Witnesses who had come out of the Imperial Club at 16–17 Duke Street said later that they had seen a woman who matched Catherine's description talking to a man on the corner of Duke Street and Church Passage. It had seemed amicable enough.

Mutilation

The unsuspecting Catherine was probably talking to Jack the Ripper. No sooner was the street empty, than her end was nigh. With no one on the scene to disturb the murderer, nothing held him back this time.

PC Edward Watkins discovered her body at 1.45 am in Mitre Square. Her mutilations were worse than in any previous case, with one deep cut severing the length of her body. Her face was badly slashed and one ear lobe had been cut through. Like the other victims of Jack the Ripper, her throat had been slit, almost certainly before the dissections began. Catherine died just three-quarters of an hour after Liz Stride; the two atrocities were dubbed 'the double murder'.

Mitre Square was a small, quiet area, accessed only by three alleys – Church Passage, leading from Duke Street, an unnamed passage, and a short alley from Mitre Street. PC Watkins discovered the body outside 8 Mitre Street, near a picture-framer's. The houses have since all been knocked down and replaced by warehouses, but the square remains.

A sketch of the dreadful murder

Police investigation

Police commissioner
Sir Charles Warren

As the body of Catherine Eddowes was found within the boundaries of the City of London, it was down to their police force to investigate the murder, not the Metropolitan police (led by the commissioner, Sir Charles Warren) who had covered the previous murders, including that of Liz Stride on the same night. There was not much to choose between the City of London police and the Metropolitan force in terms of competence. Neither had at their disposal the sort of techniques available today: there was no forensic analysis of blood groups, no fingerprinting, and no DNA testing. They relied instead on the work of Charles Warren's bloodhounds (two dogs, Burgho and Barnaby, trained to track the Ripper), witnesses, informers, reward incentives, and anything that might be revealed by an autopsy. The City police were probably a little more thorough. They took photographs of Catherine Eddowes and officers made drawings of the crime scene.

Evidence

Graffiti blaming
the Jews

The police also discovered two pieces of interesting evidence. One was a fragment of Catherine's apron, which the Ripper had used to wipe clean the blade of his knife, and which was found in a doorway in Goulston Street, off Whitechapel High Street. The second was graffiti chalked above that same doorway, saying: 'The Juwes [sic] are the Men That Will not be blamed for nothing.' The City police wanted to wait until daybreak and photograph it, but their chief officer was anxious about a negative reaction to the local Jewish community – hateful bigots were already blaming Jews for the murders – and so he ordered the graffiti to be wiped.

The 'Saucy Jacky' postcard

In a further development, the very next day (October 1) the Central News Agency received a postcard, signed Jack the Ripper. It was penned in the same handwriting as the 'Dear Boss' letter. It went as follows:

'I was not codding dear old Boss when I gave you the tip, you'll hear about Saucy Jacky's work tomorrow double event this time number one squealed a bit couldn't finish straight off. ha not the time to get ears for police. Thanks for keeping last letter back till I got to work again.

Jack the Ripper'

There is debate about the postcard's authenticity. Some say that the details of the murder described – the double event, the mutilated ear – appeared before any press release. Others maintain that a newspaper printed early on 1 October would have carried these details and therefore the postcard was a hoax. Certainly, the language betrays an assortment of styles. Some of the grammar and spelling is good, some more colloquial – perhaps to deliberately disguise the author's education.

A sample of Jack the Ripper's handwriting from one of the letters he sent

Fearful times

Understandably, there was widespread hysteria in the community about the double murder. Mass-circulation newspapers of the late Victorian period turned the Ripper case into a worldwide media frenzy. Residents bayed for the murderer's capture and became fed up with an incompetent police force. Disharmony behind the scenes at the top level in Scotland Yard did not help matters. Sir Charles Warren, commissioner of the Metropolitan police, fell out with the Home Secretary, Henry Matthews, who repeatedly refused to set a reward for information leading to the capture of the murderer. The outraged nation clamoured for a charge to be brought about. Although the public did not condemn the detective work of the police, pressure mounted on Warren, and by early November he was forced to resign.

The Whitechapel Vigilance Group

Meanwhile, the murders distracted the police from their regular duties and crime on the streets increased. A typical story in the *East End News* on 5 October reported a post office raid, with hundreds of pounds stolen. Crimes and a growing sense of insecurity prompted residents to form a voluntary vigilante group to do their own detective work. They called themselves the Whitechapel Vigilance Group and patrolled the streets, keeping an eye open for suspicious characters.

The chairman of this group was one George Lusk, who presumably became well known to the community

A knife purported to have been used by Jack the Ripper

– if he was not before. One day in mid-October, Lusk received a curious parcel. Although the publication of the Ripper correspondence had spawned a plethora of hoax letters, addressed to the police and newspaper editors, the police took this one, received by Mr Lusk, very seriously. Enclosed within a small cardboard box was half a human kidney preserved in wine, together with a note that read:

'From hell,
Mr Lusk,
Sor
I send you half the Kidne I took from one woman and prasarved it for you tother piece I fried and ate it was very nise. I may send you the bloody knif that took it out if you only wate a whil longer signed
Catch me when you can Mishter Lusk'

Cartoon of 'blind man's buff', satirizing the police

The kidney was sent to a doctor for examination and was found to be 'similar' to one removed from Catherine Eddowes's body, but no identity could be established. Apart from this unpleasant scare, no more Ripper murders happened that month. The public held its breath. An uneasy quiet fell on the night air of Whitechapel. The police were no further forward in finding their culprit.

A witness described
a man who could
have been the
murderer

The final cut: Mary Kelly

The last murder by Jack the Ripper was the most
horrific of all. Indeed, with each killing – except for
that of Liz Stride, whose murder was probably
interrupted – the atrocities became worse. The murder
of Mary Kelly was the only one indoors and for that
reason, her death was not discovered until some
considerable time after she had died. She seemed to
have the best reputation of all the victims, and was
probably the most attractive, too – tall, blue-eyed and
blonde, with a good bearing.

Life as a prostitute

Mary Kelly was born in Limerick, Ireland, and moved
to Wales with her family when young. As with many
young women of her time, she migrated to London to

find work, and after a spell as a high-class prostitute in the West End, gravitated to the East End. In 1886, she struck up with an Irish labourer, Joseph Barnett, who was living in the same lodging house in Thrawl Street, Spitalfields. They moved premises a few times, sometimes being thrown out for drunkenness. But they lived happily until he lost his job, which forced her on to the streets to work as a prostitute.

Mary started inviting homeless prostitutes to stay overnight at their home, and this Barnett did not like. After repeated arguments, he decided to leave. By this time they were living at 13 Miller's Court, off Dorset Street, which was to become Mary's fateful final address. The site was a small enclosed area, surrounded by tiny cottages and accessed only by an alley leading into Dorset Street.

Mary Kelly in Miller's Court

POLICE · BUDGET · EDITION   EDITED · BY · HAROLD · FURNISS

FAMOUS CRIMES

PAST · AND · PRESENT   ONE · PENNY

THE DISCOVERY OF THE SIXTH "RIPPER" MURDER.

Kelly meets her killer

Close to midnight, on the last night of Kelly's life, another prostitute, Mary Cox, who lived nearby, saw her talking to a shabbily dressed man in a long black coat and billycock hat. She said goodnight to Kelly, who replied that she was going to sing into the night; Mary Cox later heard her singing 'A Violet from Mother's Grave'. In the early hours of the morning a man named Hutchinson, who may have been a vigilante, noticed a man fitting the same description standing on the corner of Thrawl Street, who took Kelly by the shoulder and together they went off towards her lodgings. Hutchinson clearly took note of what he observed, including a small parcel being carried by the man.

A horrific discovery

At about 10.45 am on 9 November, the landlord's assistant went to Kelly's door at Miller's Court to collect rent. With no answer to his knocking, the boy peered through a window and saw her mutilated body. He ran to get John McCarthy, the landlord, who in turn reported the scene to the police at Commercial Street police station. On bursting into Kelly's room, detectives found her clothes neatly folded on a chair. On the bed, the near-naked body had been ripped to shreds. So horrific were the injuries that the face was said to be virtually unrecognizable. Evident, too, were all the usual features of a dismembered victim of the Ripper; only this time, the heart was missing.

> 'The face was hacked beyond recognition'
>
> **Dr Thomas Bond,**
> **post-mortem examiner**

The rent collector sees the mutilated body

The suspects

A panicking public led by a crazed media brought forth all manner of speculation about the identity of the killer. The mere fact that the bodies of the victims were heavily mutilated meant that all local butchers and slaughterers were investigated. A report of the time said that 76 such individuals were questioned. Even Queen Victoria had her say, suggesting that as the murders happened at the weekend, the culprit could be a butcher working one of the cattle boats that plied the Channel between London and Continental Europe. The docks were close to Whitechapel and the boats came in on a Thursday or Friday and left on Saturday or Sunday, which ties in with the killings happening over the weekend.

Police break open the door of Mary Kelly's lodging

A guided tour party in Ripper haunts

Doctors

Doctors Llewellyn and Phillips, who led the inquests into the deaths of Polly Nichols and Annie Chapman, considered that the removal of organs by the murderer implied surgical knowledge. A number of surgeons and doctors were therefore questioned. Even Dr Barnardo, who examined Catherine Eddowes and had spoken to her not long before she died, was on the list of suspects. But his distinctive appearance, including a heavy moustache, made him easily recognizable and so almost certainly ruled him out. However, Dr Thomas Bond, who conducted later post-mortems, dismissed the theory that the Ripper was a surgeon.

George Chapman

George Chapman (formerly Severin Klosowski) was known to be violent towards women. He was once a surgical assistant in his native Poland and worked as a hairdresser while living in Whitechapel. He became a strong suspect of the police and was hanged in 1903 for poisoning three women.

Suspect George Chapman

William Bury

William Bury was hanged in April 1889 for murdering his wife, Ellen, in Dundee, Scotland, but in 1888 he lived in nearby Bow. He moved to Scotland in January 1889. The death of Ellen, formerly a prostitute, was reminiscent of the Ripper's work. She was strangled and stabbed repeatedly in the stomach. The fact that Mary Kelly was the Ripper's final victim would tie in with Bury's departure from the East End. There was also a suggestion that the words 'Jack the Ripper is in this sellar [sic]' were chalked above the door of his home. However, the police did investigate Bury at the time but were not convinced he was the Ripper.

Nathan Kaminsky

Some detectives thought the severe manner of the killings suggested that the murderer was psychopathic. He may have been schizophrenic or an escaped lunatic. One suspect was Nathan Kaminsky, a Polish bootmaker from Whitechapel, who was known to be a violent syphilitic and was committed to Colney Hatch asylum in December 1888. His incarceration at this time would tie in with the cessation of the murders. However, he was only 23 years old, generally a lot younger than most witnesses' descriptions of the Ripper, which put him in his 30s.

Unlikely suspects

The Masonic Conspiracy centred on Albert Victor, Duke of Clarence, the eldest son of the future King Edward VII. He was said to have secretly married a Whitechapel shop assistant, Annie Crook. The exchange of vows was apparently witnessed by Mary Kelly, one of the Ripper victims, who is then said to have tried to blackmail the government with the help of other prostitutes. Prime Minister Salisbury is supposed to have ordered fellow Freemasons to track them down: the assassins are said to have included William Gull, the queen's surgeon, and the Impressionist painter Walter Sickert, who had a morbid interest in the murders and was given to indulging in self-disguise.

Other suspects include:

Montague Druitt: a teacher from Blackheath who was dismissed from school for 'serious trouble' in November 1888; soon afterwards he drowned himself in the Thames.

James Maybrick: a wealthy merchant from Liverpool whose 'diaries' are said to detail the killings, but also include proven errors.

Michael Ostrog: an intelligent Russian who trained as a doctor and had a criminal record, but no verifiable connection with the Whitechapel murders.

Albert Victor, Duke of Clarence

Conclusion

However one looks at the Ripper case, the only solid fact to emerge is that Jack the Ripper was never convicted. This very fact alone meant that investigations went on long after the murders ceased – and indeed have continued to this day. The evidence about Nathan Kaminsky, for example, came to light only in 1987, after old family notebooks were found.

Yet despite the depth and breadth of investigations, surprisingly little is known about the sort of man Jack the Ripper was. He was described as a white male of average height, who sported a moustache – in common with many Victorian men. Reports of his clothing varied, from smart to shabby, and several descriptions mentioned a deerstalker or billycock hat. He probably lived locally, for all the murders happened within a square mile. But what was his motive? Was he a

From Hell, a film about Jack the Ripper, starred Johnny Depp

psychopathic loner with a hatred of women? Did he harbour a grievance about prostitutes, perhaps as a result of some past humiliation? We know that prostitutes habitually lured men into dark alleys for their business, and so made his job quite easy.

Questions like these are still being asked. Although Jack the Ripper was not the first serial killer in history, he was the first to come under the spotlight of mass-circulation newspapers, which had begun only recently. It is no wonder that the Ripper case caught the public imagination throughout the world, inspiring books, films and plays ever since the events took place.

Areas associated with the Whitechapel murders

Districts: Whitechapel, Spitalfields, Aldgate, Commercial Road, Commercial Street, Whitechapel High Street, Middlesex Street (formerly Petticoat Lane), Brick Lane

Emma Smith
- Farrance Street, Limehouse – *Emma seen with a man on the night of her murder.*
- Junction of Brick Lane and Osborn Street (**1** on map overleaf) – *Emma attacked near here.*
- London Hospital, Whitechapel Road (**2**) – *Emma died here.*

Martha Tabram
- Leadenhall Street, near Aldgate pump (**3**) – *Martha seen destitute.*
- Angel Alley (**4**) – *Pearly Poll and guardsman had sex.*
- Gunthorpe Street (formerly George Yard) (**5**) – *Martha was murdered.*

Mary Ann (Polly) Nichols
- Surviving buildings of Lambeth workhouse, Renfrew Road – *Polly lived at the workhouse after her marriage ended.*
- 'Ingleside', Rosehill Road, Wandsworth – *Polly was a servant to the Cowdrys, who lived here.*
- 18 Thrawl Street, Spitalfields (**6**) – *Polly's lodging house.*
- 13 Brick Lane, site of the Frying Pan pub, on corner of Thrawl Street and Brick Lane (**7**) – *Polly seen here on the night she died.*
- South side of Durward Street, Whitechapel (formerly Buck's Row) (**8**) – *Polly's body found.*

Annie Chapman
- Unnamed private road (formerly Dorset Street) (**9**) between Commercial Street and Crispin Street (near Fashion Street), Spitalfields, with car park on the south side and warehouses on the north side – *Site of Crossingham's Lodging House, 35 Dorset Street – Annie lodged here.*
- Brushfield Street to Spitalfields Market (**10**) – *Part of the route taken by Annie on her last night.*
- Truman's Brewery, Hanbury Street (**11**) – *Built on site of houses including number 29, where Annie was murdered.*
- Residential block, Commercial Street (by Fleur De Lis Street), the former Commercial Street Police Station (**12**)– *Police from here went to investigate the murder.*
- 22 Mulberry Street (**13**) – *Home address of John 'Leather Apron' Pizer.*
- Fleet Street – *Site of the Central News Agency (precise address unknown), which received the 'Dear Boss' letter.*
- Scotland Yard – *At the time of the murders in 1888, the headquarters of the Metropolitan Police was located at 4 Whitehall Place (running between Whitehall*

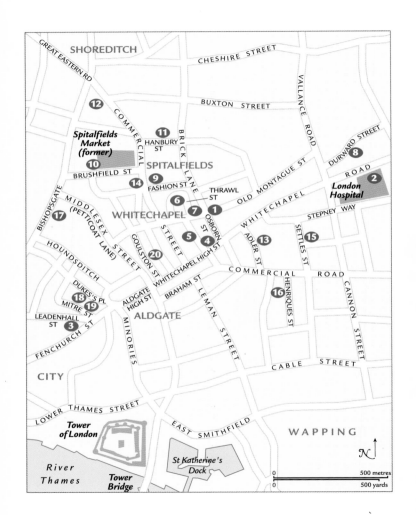

SHOREDITCH

CHESHIRE STREET

GREAT EASTERN RD

VALLANCE ROAD

BUXTON STREET

DURWARD STREET

12

COMMERCIAL

8

Spitalfields
Market
(former)

11

HANBURY
ST

ROAD

BRICK LANE

10

BRUSHFIELD ST

SPITALFIELDS

London
Hospital

2

14

9

FASHION ST

THRAWL
ST

OLD MONTAGUE ST

STEPNEY WAY

6

BISHOPSGATE

17

MIDDLESEX

7

WHITECHAPEL

OSBORN ST

WHITECHAPEL

STREET

(PETTICOAT LANE)

5

4

ADLER ST

13

SETTLES ST

15

HOUNDSDITCH

STREET

GOULSTON ST

20

WHITECHAPEL HIGH ST

COMMERCIAL

ROAD

CANNON

BRAHAM ST

HENRIQUES ST

16

DUKES'S PL

18

MITRE

19

ALDGATE
HIGH ST

LEMAN STREET

STREET

LEADENHALL
ST

3

FENCHURCH ST

ALDGATE

MINORIES

CABLE STREET

CITY

LOWER THAMES STREET

EAST SMITHFIELD

WAPPING

Tower
of London

N

0   500 metres

River
Thames

Tower
Bridge

St Katherine's
Dock

0   500 yards

and Northumberland Ave). The building (now demolished) backed on to Greater Scotland Yard. The police remained here until 1890, when they moved to New Scotland Yard on the Embankment. While the Ripper murders were being committed, this new edifice was still in the process of being built.

Old shop front in Spitalfields

Elizabeth (Liz) Stride

● The Workhouse leisure centre, Poplar High Street, site of Poplar workhouse – *Liz stayed here.*
● 74 Commercial Street (formerly the Queen's Head pub) (**14**) – *A common haunt.*
● 34 Settles Street (running north off Commercial Road), formerly the Bricklayer's Arms pub (**15**) – *Liz sighted here on her last night, arm in arm with a man who was possibly the Ripper.*
● Henriques Street (formerly Berner Street) (**16**) – *Liz's body found at Dutfield's Yard, 40 Berner Street.*
● East London Cemetery, Plaistow, London E13. Grave 15509, square 37 – *Burial place of Elizabeth Stride, 1843–88. Buried Saturday 6 October 1888.*

Catherine Eddowes

● 182 Bishopsgate, Bishopsgate Police Station (site of earlier building) (**17**) – *Catherine was locked up for being drunk and abusive on the night she died.*
● Corner of Duke's Place (formerly Duke Street) and St James's Passage (formerly Church Passage) (**18**)– *Catherine seen talking to a man.*
● Mitre Square (**19**) – *The murder scene.*
● Goulston Street, off Whitechapel High Street (**20**) – *Fragment of Catherine's apron found in a doorway, with anti-Semitic graffiti above.*
● Memorial site at City of London Cemetery, Ilford – *Memorial gardens with a commemorative plaque to Catherine, memorial bed 1849.*

Mary Kelly

● Unnamed private road (formerly Dorset Street) (**9**) between Commercial Street and Crispin Street (near Fashion Street), Spitalfields – *Miller's Court, site of Mary's murder, was off this road on the north side.*

First published in the United Kingdom in 2011 by
Batsford, 10 Southcombe Street, London W14 0RA
An imprint of Anova Books Company Ltd

Copyright © Batsford 2011

All rights reserved. No part of this publication may be reproduced, stored in a
retrieval system, or transmitted in any form or by any means, electronic,
mechanical, photocopying, recording or otherwise, without the prior written
permission of the copyright owner.

ISBN: 978 1 906388 95 9
A CIP catalogue record for this book is available from the British Library.

18 17 16 15 14 13 12 11
10 9 8 7 6 5 4 3 2 1

Reproduction by Rival Colour Ltd, UK
Printed by 1010 Printing Ltd, China

This book can be ordered direct from the publisher at the website
www.anovabooks.co.uk, or try your local bookshop.

Picture credits

page 1 © Jaspa Photography / Alamy; 2 (left) © Mary Evans Picture Library / Alamy; (right)
© Mary Evans Picture Library / Alamy; 3 (top and bottom) © The Print Collector / Alamy;
4 © The Art Archive / Alamy; 5 © Mary Evans Picture Library / Alamy; 6-7 © Alan King
engraving / Alamy; 8 Mary Evans Picture Library; 10-11 © Gary Roebuck / Alamy;
12 © Johnny Jones / Alamy; 13 © INTERFOTO / Alamy; 14-15 © The Print Collector /
Alamy; 17 © INTERFOTO / Alamy; 18 © Toby de Silva / Alamy; 19 © Mary Evans Picture
Library / Alamy; 20 © Trinity Mirror / Mirrorpix / Alamy; 21 © Toby de Silva / Alamy;
22 © Mary Evans Picture Library / Alamy; 23 © INTERFOTO / Alamy; 24-25 © Illustrated
London News Ltd/Mary Evans; 26 (top) © Trinity Mirror / Mirrorpix / Alamy; (bottom)
© Pictorial Press Ltd / Alamy; 26-27 © Mary Evans Picture Library / Alamy; 28 © Toby de
Silva / Alamy; 28-29 (background) © Toby de Silva / Alamy; 30 © Mary Evans Picture
Library / Alamy; 31 Mary Evans Picture Library/DAVID LEWIS HODGSON; 32 (top)
© Classic Image / Alamy; (bottom) © Mary Evans Picture Library / Alamy; 33 Mary Evans
Picture Library/DAVID LEWIS HODGSON; 34 Mary Evans Picture Library/DONALD
RUMBELOW; 35 (top) Mary Evans Picture Library; (bottom) © Mary Evans Picture Library
/ Alamy; 36 © Mary Evans Picture Library / Alamy; 37 *A Lost Woman, Mary Kelly, in Miller's
Court*, 1888 (engraving) (b&w photo) by English School, (19th century) Private Collection/
The Bridgeman Art Library; 38 and 39 © Mary Evans Picture Library / Alamy; 40 © Mary
Evans Picture Library / Alamy; 41 © David Pearson / Alamy; 42 © Trinity Mirror / Mirrorpix
/ Alamy; 43 © Mary Evans Picture Library / Alamy; 44 (background) © Mary Evans Picture
Library / Alamy; (inset) © MovieMagic / Alamy; 47 © Steve Ullathorne / Alamy.
Map on page 46 courtesy of Martin Brown Design.